Paper Animals
IN ACTION!

Clothespins Make the Models Move!

Rob Ives

Dover Publications, Inc.
Mineola, New York

Bibliographical Note

Paper Animals in Action! is a new work, first published by Dover Publications, Inc., in 2019.

International Standard Book Number
ISBN-13: 978-0-486-83591-4
ISBN-10: 0-486-83591-X

Manufactured in the United States by LSC Communications
83591X01
www.doverpublications.com

2 4 6 8 10 9 7 5 3 1

2019

Contents

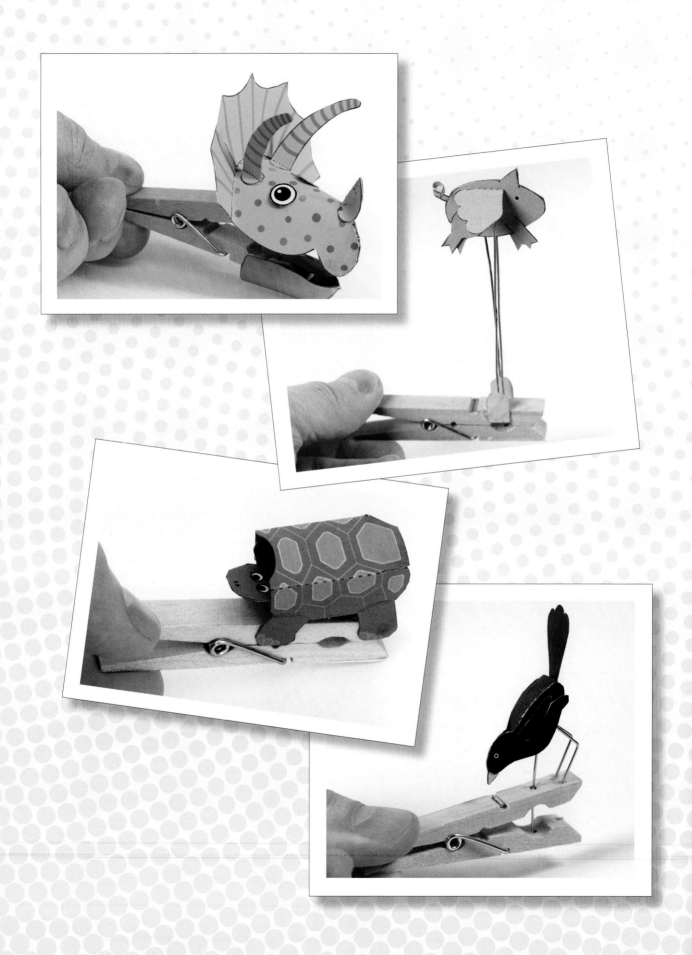

Introduction
Clothespin Automata

Automata are moving models that aim to bring otherwise static sculptures to life. The original automata from years gone by were made from leather, wood, and brass. The projects in this book are for you to cut out and assemble. With clothespin automata, the main materials are paper parts from this book, paper clips, and clothespins!

With just a few items you'll find in your "making" drawer, you will be able to follow the fully illustrated instructions and create 12 unique moving paper models, each of which will bring a different animal to life. You will use a variety of different mechanisms to make the models— a great introduction to STEM education!

You will need the following supplies: wire paper clips, wooden clothespins, round toothpicks, Popsicle® sticks, a small lollipop with a hollow tube (e.g., Chupa Chups®), and the parts from this book.

You will need the following tools: scissors, a ruler, a craft knife, a cutting mat, a power drill with 1/8" (3 mm) and 5/64" (2 mm) drill bits, needle-nose pliers, wire cutter (or side cutter) pliers, white school glue (e.g., Elmer's®), and waste wood. A glue spreader is helpful, although a coffee stirrer or a Popsicle stick will also work well.

Note: This book requires the use of power drills, craft knives, and other tools that can cause injury if users aren't careful. Readers are encouraged to remain alert, exercise caution, and follow all safety procedures. Children should not use power drills, craft knives, and other potentially dangerous tools without adult guidance and supervision.

General Instructions
For All Models

- The parts mentioned in the steps refer to the model parts in the back of the book. Each project mentions the page number for the corresponding model parts.

- Before cutting, review the project. Take some time to read through all the instructions and look at the photographs. When you are ready, remove the pages from the back section of the book.

- Using the point of the scissors and ruler, carefully score along the dotted and dashed lines. These lines mark the folds in the model, and scoring will help make these folds crisp and accurate. Once you have scored all the dotted and dashed lines, use the craft knife to cut out any holes or small areas in the model pieces.

- Dotted lines show valley folds, and dashed lines are mountain folds. Cut out any holes before carefully cutting out the parts.

- The gray areas indicate where to glue. The gray areas are only marked on the front side of the model sheets.

- Before assembling the model, spend some time folding all the crease lines to ensure that they are nice and crisp.

- Use glue sparingly on one side of the joint only. After you have joined the pieces together, make sure that they are lined up accurately. Then pinch them together to seal the joint.

- Take care at each stage! The more care and accuracy you use when you make these models, the better they will work and the better they will look.

Paper Animals
IN ACTION!

Talking Triceratops

Squeeze the clothespin closed, and the triceratops
opens her mouth to talk! See page 57.

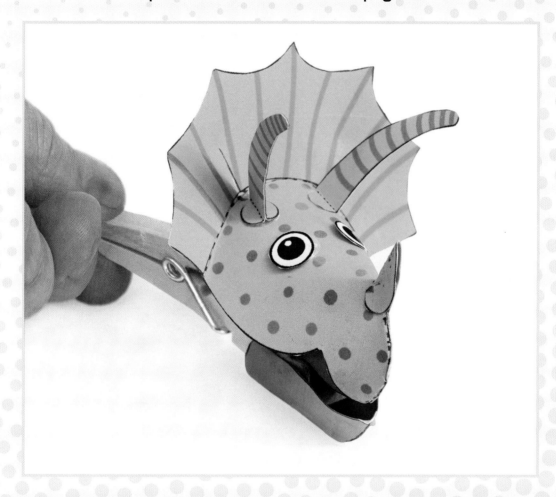

You will need:

• 1 wooden clothespin

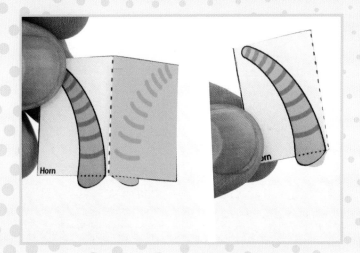

Step 1: Fold over the horns, and glue them down to make a double thickness card. Set them aside to dry.

Step 2: Glue the head—inner to the underside of the head—top.

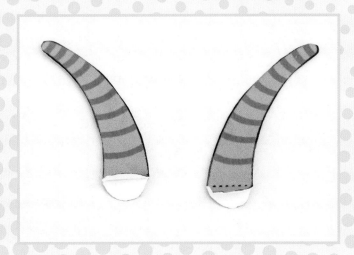

Step 3: Carefully cut out the horns.

Step 4: Glue together the tabs that make the snout.

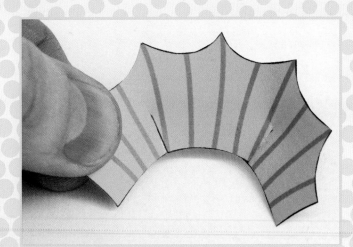

Step 5: Glue up the two darts in the frill.

Step 6: Glue the frill to the head.

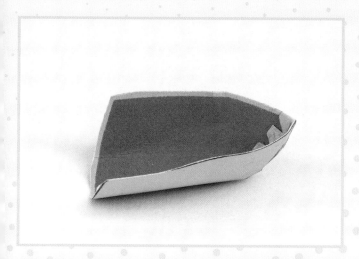

Step 7: Glue the end of the lower jaw together.

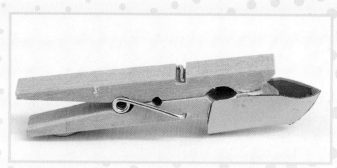

Step 8: Glue the lower jaw of the triceratops to the lower jaw of the clothespin.

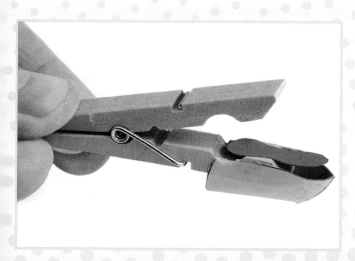

Step 9: Glue the tongue to the top of the clothespin's lower jaw.

Step 10: Glue the head—inner to the upper jaw of the clothespin.

Step 11: Glue the eyes and the three horns into place.

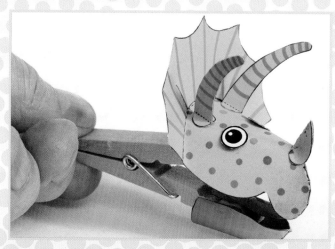

Step 12: Squeeze the clothespin to open the triceratops's mouth. Roar!

Flying Pig

This porker flaps his wings to fly,
using linkages and pushrods! See page 59.

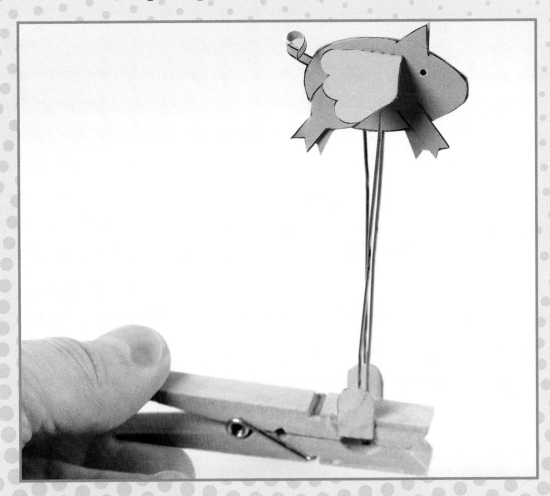

You Will need:

- 1 wooden clothespin
- 1 wire paper clip

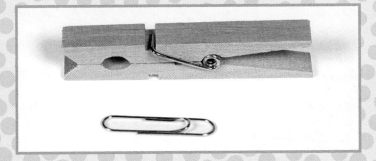

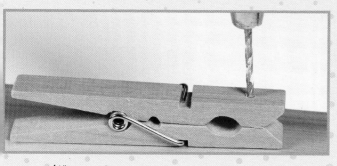

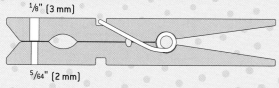

1/8" (3 mm)

5/64" (2 mm)

Step 1: Use the clothespin template to mark where the hole in the clothespin will go. Place the clothespin on a piece of waste wood so that you do not damage the worktop. Drill down through the clothespin using a 5/64" (2 mm) drill. Drill again with a 1/8" (3 mm) drill, only through the top jaw of the clothespin.

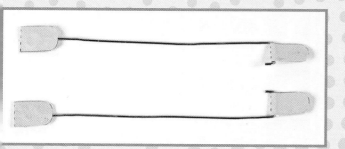

Step 3: Fold over and glue down the end tabs to sandwich the circle ends of the wing wires. Fold the wing tabs in half, and glue them into place to make hinges.

Step 5: Fit the circle of the body pushrod into the circle pocket, and glue on the other side of the body—outer. Lift the legs slightly clear of the body to give them some depth.

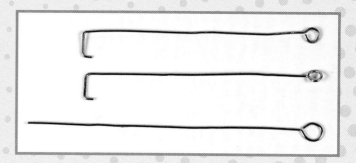

Step 2: Straighten the wires, and bend them into shape to fit the templates using a pair of needle-nose pliers.

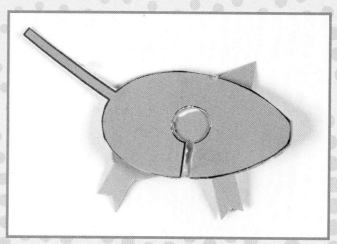

Step 4: Glue together one side of the body—outer and two body—inner layers.

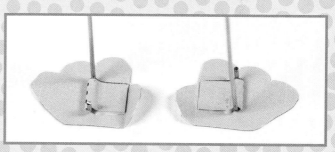

Step 6: Glue the wing tabs to the underside of the wings so that they touch the hinge crease line.

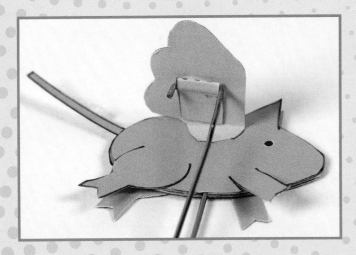

Step 8: Thread the body wire down through the hole on the clothespin and out the other side.

Step 7: Glue the wings to the body.

Step 10: With the wings down, bend the body wire along the underside of the clothespin's lower jaw. Use wire cutters to cut off any excess wire, leaving a piece about 1/8" (3 mm) long.

Step 9: Glue the two ends of the wing pushrods to the sides of the clothespin's upper jaw.

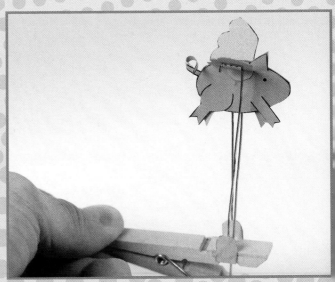

Step 11: Use a craft knife to scrape a shallow trough in the clothespin to house the wire, and glue the cover into place.

Step 12: Give the pig's tail a curl. Then it is ready to fly! Squeeze the clothespin to flap the wings.

Flying Goose

Turn the crank handle, and the goose rocks back and forth and flies!
See page 61.

You will need:

- 1 wooden clothespin
- 5 wire paper clips
- 2 Popsicle sticks
- 1 small lollipop with a hollow tube

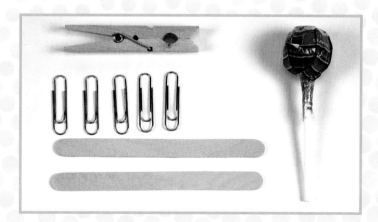

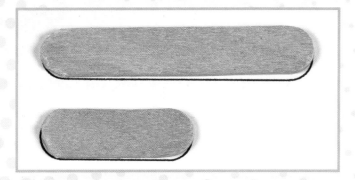

Step 1: Use the template to cut the Popsicle sticks to size.

Step 2: Drill three 5/64" (2 mm) holes into the longer Popsicle stick using the template as a guide.

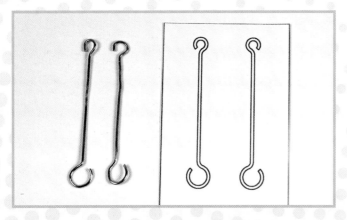

Step 3: Straighten two of the wire paper clips. Then use a pair of needle-nose pliers to shape them the same as the template. Use wire cutters to cut off any excess wire.

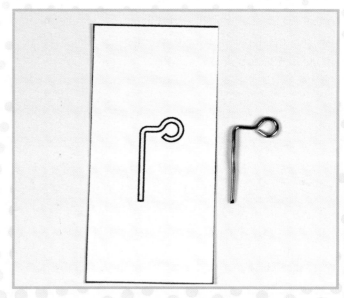

Step 4: Straighten a wire paper clip. Then use a pair of needle-nose pliers to shape it the same as the template. Use wire cutters to cut off any excess wire.

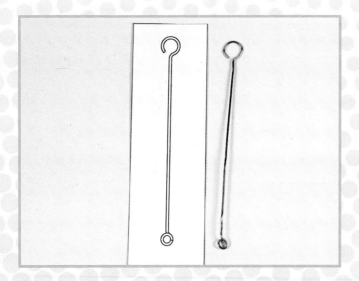

Step 5: Straighten a wire paper clip. Then use a pair of needle-nose pliers to shape it the same as the template. Use wire cutters to cut off any excess wire.

Step 6: Cut off 3/16" (5 mm) from the lollipop stick.

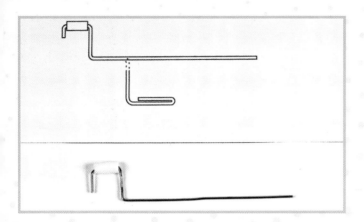

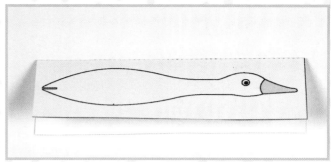

Step 7: Straighten a wire paper clip. Then use a pair of needle-nose pliers to shape it the same as the template. Thread the plastic tube from the lollipop stick onto the wire, and bend the end over, trapping it into place. It should be free to spin on the wire.

Step 8: Fold the body of the goose in half without gluing it.

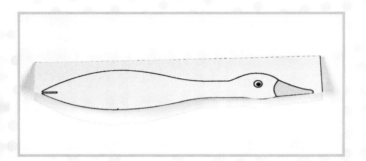

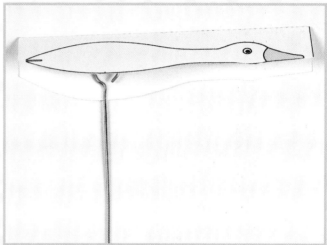

Step 9: Still without gluing, cut along the bottom of the body on both sides.

Step 10: Fit the wide loop from Step 5 into the body, and glue it down.

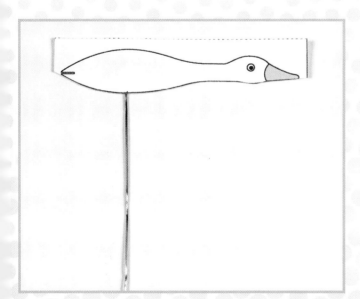

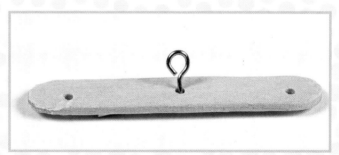

Step 12: Thread the wire from Step 4 into the center hole of the Popsicle stick.

Step 11: Make sure that the body is flat while the glue dries.

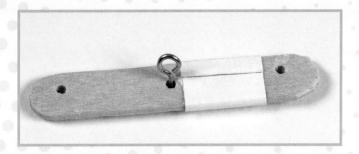

Step 13: Tightly glue and wrap the paper tab around the wire to secure it into position.

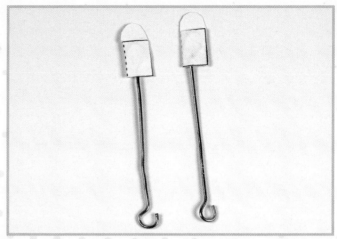

Step 14: Glue the wing tabs to the wires from Step 3.

Step 15: Cut the rest of the body out.

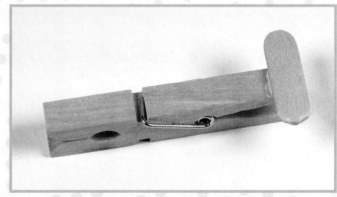

Step 16: Glue the smaller Popsicle stick to the end of the clothespin.

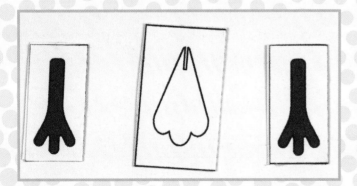

Step 17: Glue the feet and tails over to make a double thickness card.

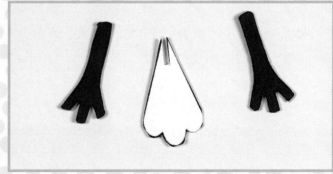

Step 18: Once the glue is dry, carefully cut them out.

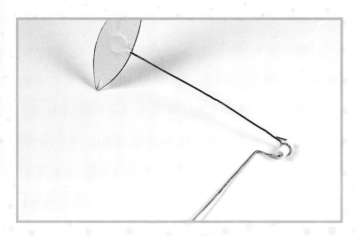

Step 19: Wrap the end of the long body wire around the tube from the lollipop stick, and make sure it is tight.

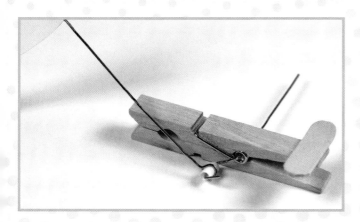

Step 21: Thread the crank through the axle.

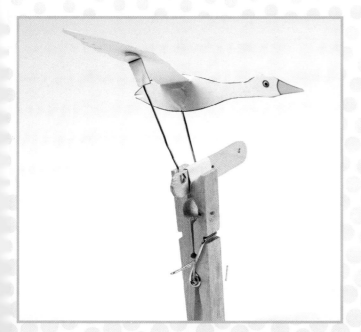

Step 23: Glue the wings to the body. Connect the body to the Popsicle stick with the wire linkages.

Step 20: Roll the paper axle, and fit it into the clothespin.

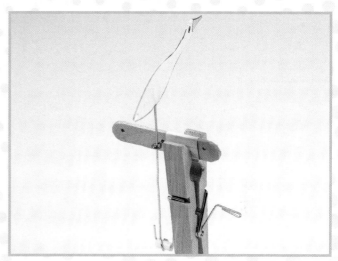

Step 22: Fit the pushrod wire through the loop on the Popsicle stick. Grip the Popsicle stick in the jaws of the clothespin. Shape the rest of the crank wire to make a handle.

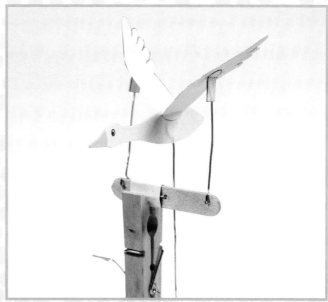

Step 24: Repeat with the other wing. Glue on the feet and slot in the tail. Squeeze the clothespin to make the wings flap.

Nodding Dog

The linkage under the dog's chin makes her nod her head!
See page 63.

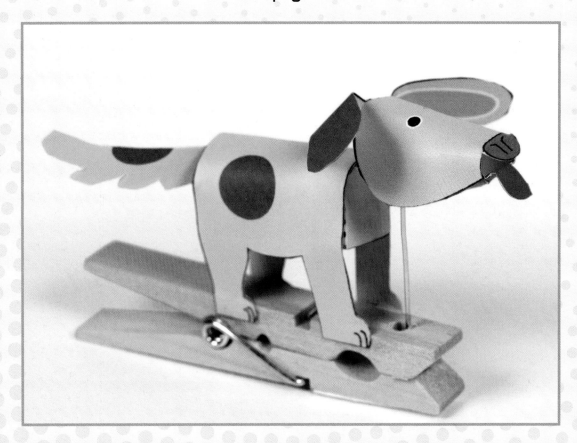

You will need:

- 1 wooden clothespin

- 1 wire paper clip

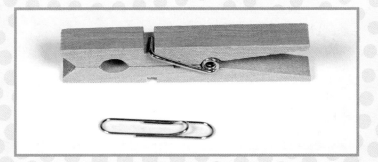

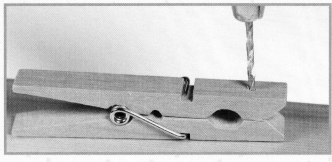

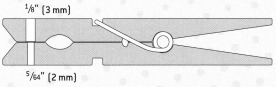

1/8" (3 mm)

5/64" (2 mm)

Step 1: Use the clothespin template to mark where the hole in the clothespin will go. Place the clothespin on a piece of waste wood so that you do not damage the worktop. Drill down through the clothespin with a 5/64" (2 mm) drill. Drill again, but this time with a 1/8" (3 mm) drill and only through the top jaw of the clothespin.

Step 2: Fold over and glue the tail. Don't glue the semicircular tabs.

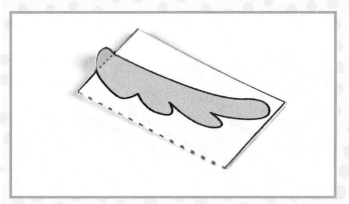

Step 3: Set it aside, and let the glue dry.

Step 4: Fold over the tab on the body—front, and glue it down to make the head support double thickness.

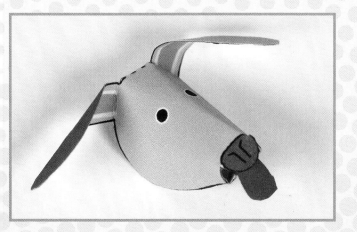

Step 5: Fold around and glue the head. Gently curve and shape the ears and tongue.

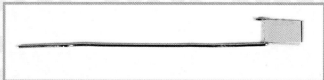

Step 6: Straighten a wire paper clip. Then use a pair of needle-nose pliers to shape it the same as the template. Fold the head tab over, and glue it to the end of the wire.

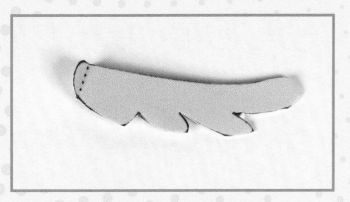

Step 7: Once the glue is dry, cut out the tail.

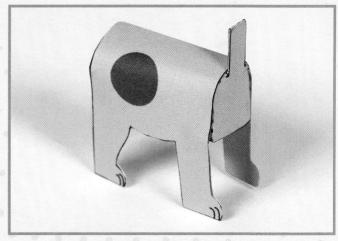

Step 8: Fit the body—front into the body.

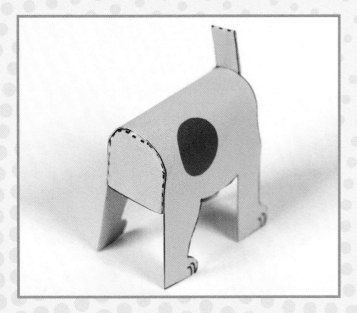

Step 9: Fit the body—back into the body.

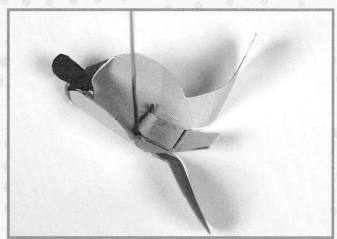

Step 10: Glue the pushrod tab into the inside of the head.

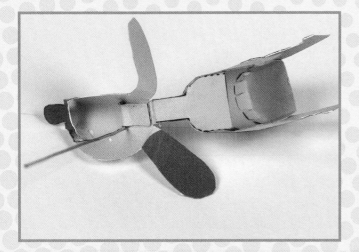

Step 11: Glue the head to the head stand on the body.

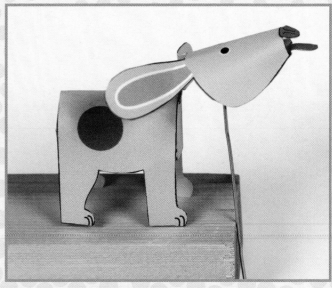

Step 12: The body and head are glued together.

Step 13: Glue the tail into place.

Step 14: Thread the wire down through the larger hole in the clothespin and out through the smaller hole. Glue the feet to the sides of the clothespin.

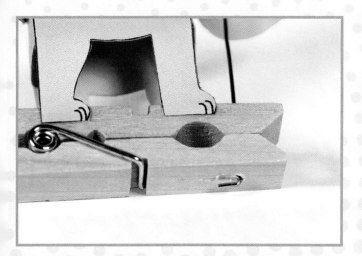

Step 15: With the head in an upright position, bend the wire along the bottom of the clothespin. Use wire cutters to cut off all but a small length of wire.

Step 16: Use a craft knife to scrape a small trough in the underside of the clothespin. Set the wire in the trough, and secure it in position with the cover piece.

Step 17: Squeeze the clothespin to make the dog nod.

Pecking Bird

A simple linkage and hinge bring the blackbird to life,
making him bob and peck! See page 65.

You will need:

- 1 wooden clothespin
- 2 wire paper clips
- 2 round toothpicks

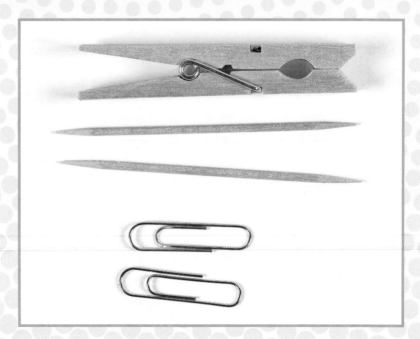

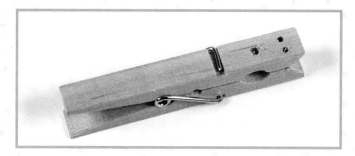

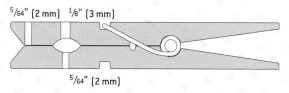

5/64" (2 mm)   1/8" (3 mm)

5/64" (2 mm)

Step 1: Use the template to drill the holes in the clothespin. Drill a 5/64" (2 mm) hole all the way through. Then drill a 1/8" (3 mm) hole through the upper jaw only. The other two holes are 5/64" (2 mm) in diameter and should go through the upper jaw of the clothespin only.

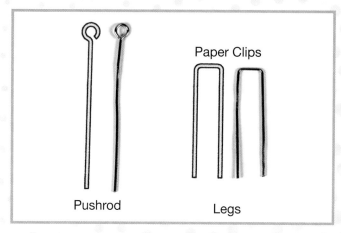

Paper Clips

Pushrod   Legs

Step 2: Straighten out the paper clips. Then shape them to the templates using a pair of needle-nose pliers.

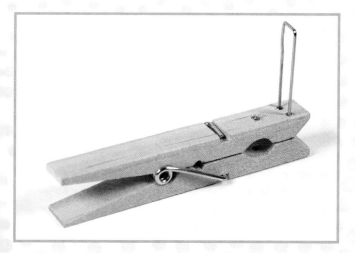

Step 3: Fit the leg wire into the clothespin.

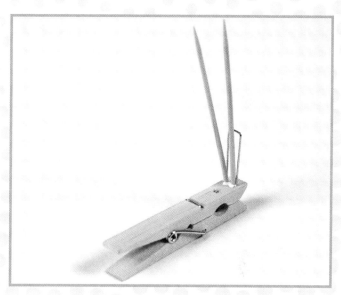

Step 4: Glue the ends of the toothpicks. Then push them in with the wire to wedge the wire into place.

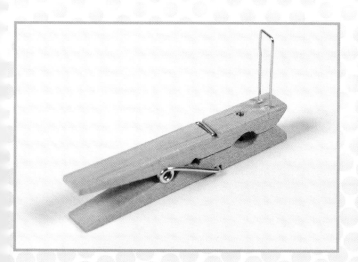

Step 5: Cut off any excess toothpick.

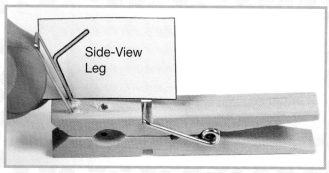

Side-View Leg

Step 6: Use the side template to bend the legs backward . . .

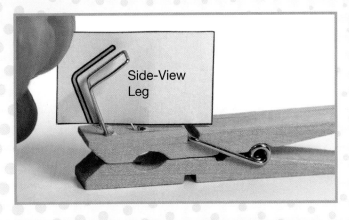

Side-View Leg

Step 7: . . . and forward to shape the legs.

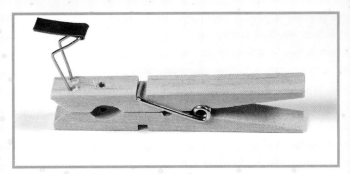

Step 8: Fold the hinge piece in half, and glue it over the wire.

Step 9: Thread a toothpick through the pushrod wire. Then thread the wire down through the slot in the body—inner.

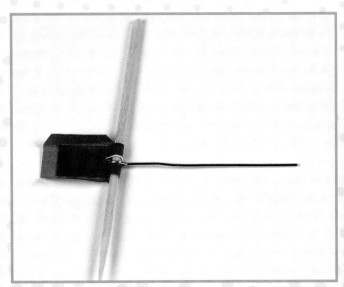

Step 10: Fold the body—inner over, gluing it to the toothpick.

Step 11: Cut off any excess toothpick from either side of the body—inner.

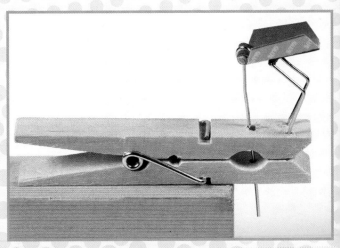

Step 12: Thread the wire down through the hole in the clothespin, and glue the body—inner to the hinge.

Step 13: Glue the head—inner to the inside of the body.

Step 14: Glue the other side of the body into place. Only glue the head.

Step 15: Glue the body to the body—inner.

Step 16: Glue the tail into place on the body—inner.

Step 17: Glue the body—back into place.

Step 18: With the bird in an upright position, bend the wire along the bottom of the clothespin. Use wire cutters to cut off most of the wire, except about 1/8" (3 mm).

Step 19: Use a craft knife to scrape a shallow trough in the clothespin to house the wire. Then secure it into place with the cover piece.

Step 20: Glue on the wings.

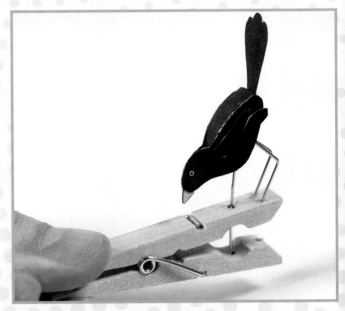

Step 21: Squeeze the clothespin to make the bird peck.

Surprised Penguin

As the clothespin is operated, the cute penguin raises her wings in surprise! See page 67.

You will need:

- 1 wooden clothespin
- 1 wire paper clip

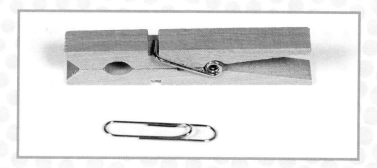

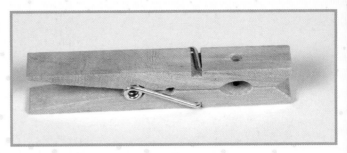

Step 2: The drilled clothespin is ready for building!

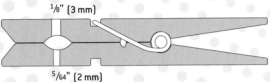

¹⁄₈" (3 mm)

⁵⁄₆₄" (2 mm)

Step 1: Use the clothespin template to mark where the hole in the clothespin will go. Place the clothespin on a piece of waste wood so that you do not damage the worktop. Drill down all the way through the clothespin with a 5/64" (2 mm) drill. Drill again, but this time with a 1/8" drill (3 mm) and only through the top jaw of the clothespin.

Step 3: Glue the inside of the wing, and fold the card down to make a double thickness card.

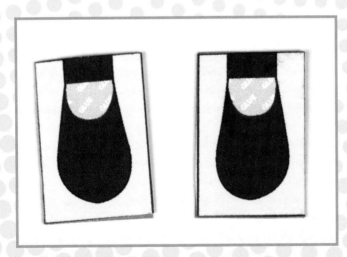

Step 4: Repeat with the other wing.

Step 5: Once the glue is dry, carefully cut out the wings.

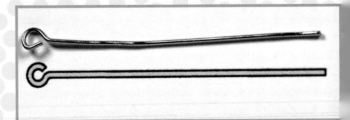

Step 6: Straighten a wire paper clip. Then use a pair of needle-nose pliers to shape it the same as the template. Use wire cutters to cut off any excess wire.

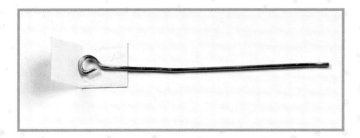

Step 7: Glue the tab over the end of the wire, and glue it down.

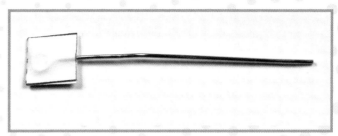

Step 8: Squeeze the tabs tight, and let the glue dry.

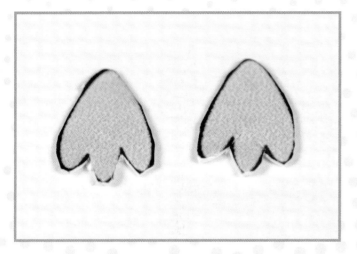

Step 9: Assemble the feet from a double thickness card.

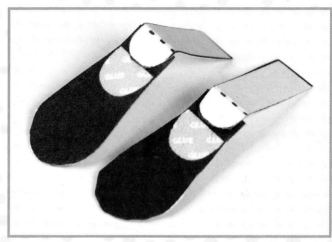

Step 10: Glue the pull tabs to the wings.

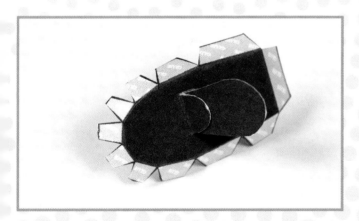

Step 11: Thread the wing through the body, and glue it to the semicircular tab.

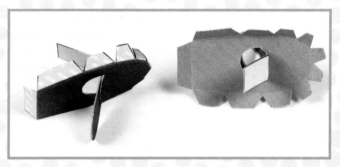

Step 12: Repeat with the other wing.

Step 13: Glue the front of the body to the sides.

Step 14: Glue the wire tab to one of the wing pull tabs. Line up the bottom of both parts.

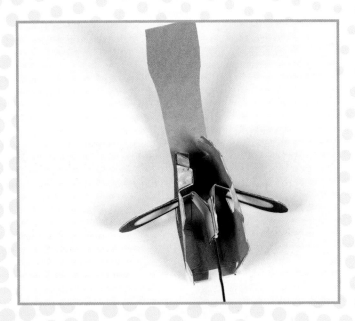

Step 15: Once the glue has dried on the first pull tab, glue the other pull tab to the other side and let the glue dry.

Step 16: Glue the rest of the body and side together. Once the glue is dry, pull the wire to raise the wings.

Step 17: Glue on the beak.

Step 18: Glue on the feet.

Step 19: Thread the wire down through the large hole and out through the bottom of the clothespin. Glue the body to the clothespin.

Step 20: With the wings in their down position, bend the wire over to 90°.

Step 21: Use wire cutters to cut off the wire, leaving about 1/8" (3 mm). Use a craft knife to scrape a little trough in the clothespin to house the wire.

Step 22: Glue the cover into place to trap the wire.

Step 23: Let the glue dry completely.

Step 24: Squeeze the clothespin to raise the wings!

Flapping Butterfly

Squeeze the clothespin, and the butterfly spreads her wings out to all their beautiful glory! See page 69.

You will need:

- 1 wooden clothespin
- 2 round toothpicks
- 4 wire paper clips

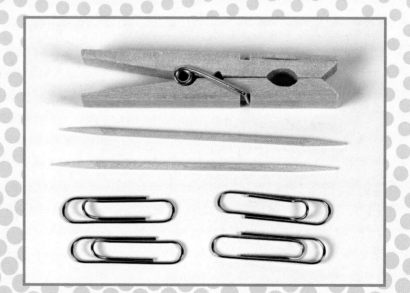

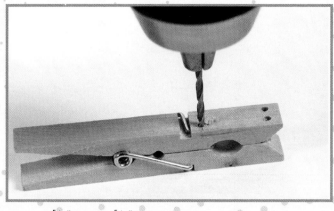

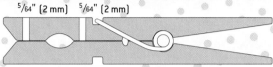

Step 1: Use the template to mark the four holes in the clothespin.

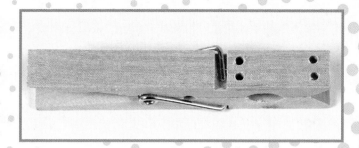

Step 2: The four holes should be 5/64" (2 mm) in diameter and should go through the top jaw only.

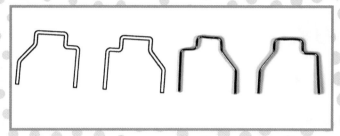

Step 4: Straighten out the other two paper clips, and shape the legs to match the leg templates.

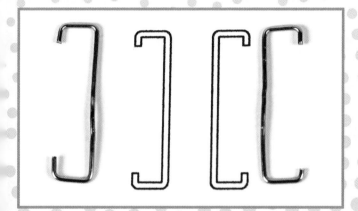

Step 3: Straighten out two paper clips. Make the wing pushrods, using the templates as a guide.

Step 6: Lay the upper wings on top, and glue them to the lower wings where they overlap.

Step 5: Lay the lower wings onto the wing template.

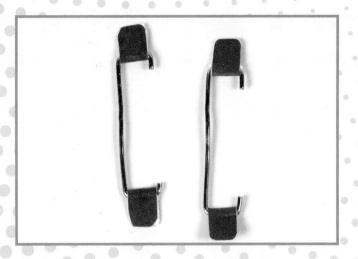

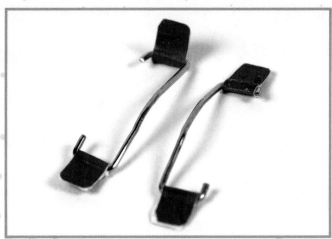

Step 7: Fold the pushrod tabs in half, and glue them to the wing pushrods.

Step 8: Curve the wing pushrods up slightly. This will give the clearance around the clothespin.

Step 9: Bend the tabs round, and glue the wings to the legs. They should be free to "flap."

Step 10: For each wing, fold the body link around the top straight section of the legs. Glue it down, being careful not to stick it to the wing. The wing must be free to move.

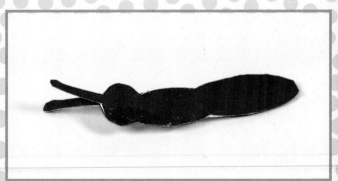

Step 11: Let the glue dry completely.

Step 12: Glue together the two halves of the body. Keep the antennae unglued.

Step 13: Fit the legs into the holes in the clothespin.

Step 14: Glue the ends of the toothpick, and jam them into the holes with the wire legs to wedge them into place.

Step 15: Cut off any excess toothpick.

Step 16: Fit the body between the wings, and glue it to the body links. Don't get any glue on the wings!

Step 17: Glue one end of the wing pushrod to the bottom jaw of the clothespin and the other end to the wing. Do this on both sides. Let the glue dry.

Step 18: Squeeze the clothespin to open the wings.

Brave Turtle

Open the clothespin, and watch the turtle poke his head out of his shell!
See page 71.

You will need:

- 1 wooden clothespin
- 1 wire paper clip

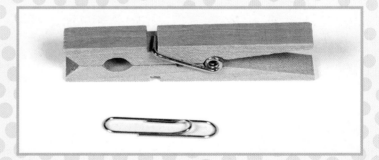

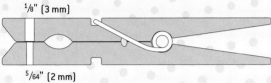

1/8" (3 mm)

5/64" (2 mm)

Step 1: Use the template to mark where the hole goes in the clothespin. Drill through the clothespin with a 2 mm (5/64") drill bit. Then drill the top jaw only with a 3 mm (1/8") bit.

Step 3: Fold over the base tab to trap the end of the wire.

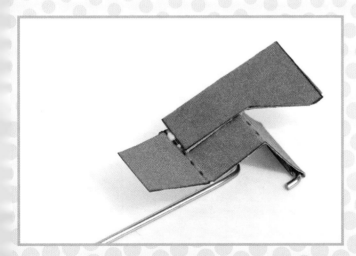

Step 5: Glue one of the Stage One pieces to the base, lining up the edge with the center line.

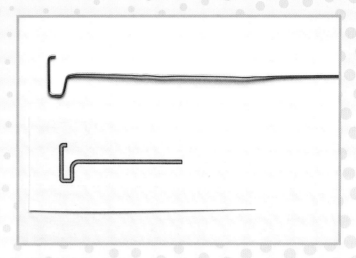

Step 2: Straighten out the paper clip. Use pliers to shape the paper clip to match the template.

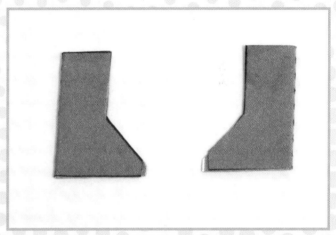

Step 4: Fold over and glue the two Stage One pieces to make a double thickness card.

Step 6: Glue the other Stage One piece into place, making a cross.

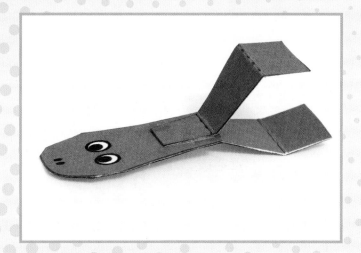

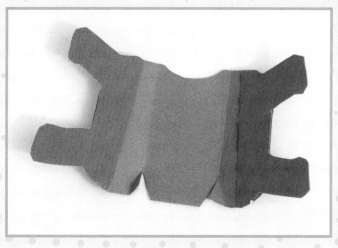

Step 7: Glue the Stage Two pieces to the front and back of the head.

Step 8: Glue the legs to the inside of the shell. Carefully line them up with the edge of the shell.

Step 10: Glue the Stage Two pieces to the Stage One pieces.

Step 9: Fold and glue the tabs.

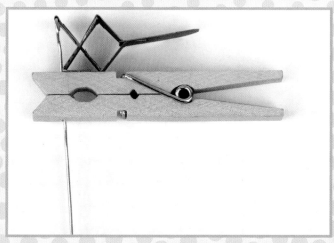

Step 12: Glue the base tab to the clothespin so that it touches the wire.

Step 11: Thread the wire down through the hole in the clothespin.

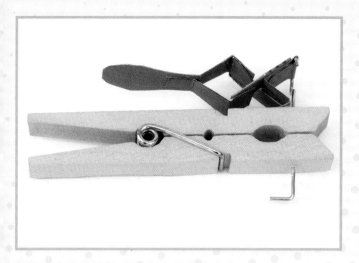

Step 13: Fold over the wire and cut.

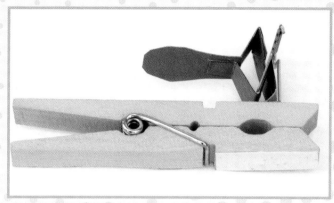

Step 14: Scratch a shallow groove in the clothespin. Cover the groove with the cover piece to secure it into place.

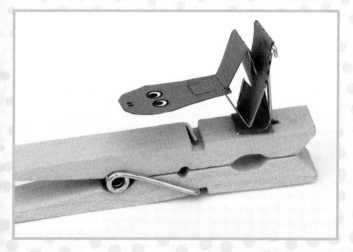

Step 15: Test the mechanism by squeezing the clothespin.

Step 16: Glue the legs to the side of the clothespin.

Step 17: Squeeze the clothespin, and the turtle sticks his head out of his shell.

Stretching Moose

Open the clothespin to make the moose stretch his neck and body!
See page 75.

You will need:

- 1 wooden clothespin
- 1 wire paper clip

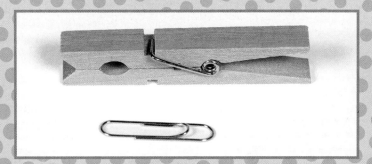

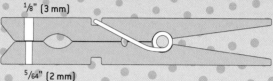

1/8" (3 mm)

5/64" (2 mm)

Step 1: Use the template to mark where the hole goes in the clothespin. Drill through the clothespin with a 2 mm (5/64") drill bit. Then drill the top jaw only with a 3 mm (1/8") bit.

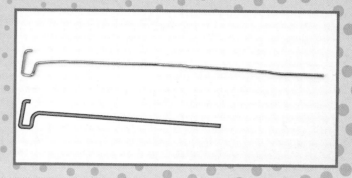

Step 2: Straighten out the paper clip. Use pliers to shape the paper clip to match the template.

Step 4: Fold around and glue the legs.

Step 3: Fold the wire end over the wire, and glue it down.

Step 6: Glue the body stand into the legs, lining it up with the gray lines on the legs.

Step 5: Fold over and glue the body stand back to back, leaving the tabs unglued.

Step 7: Fold over and glue the link to make a double thickness card.

Step 8: Assemble the body—outer. Glue on the tail.

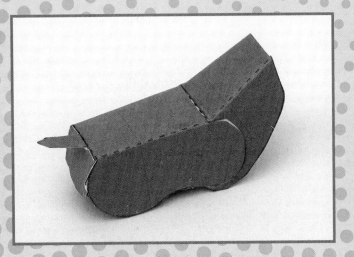

Step 9: Glue the neck into place.

Step 10: Assemble the head. Glue on the antlers.

Step 11: Glue the wire. Bend the wire to the inside of the neck so that it is lined up with the point where the neck and body meet.

Step 12: Glue the link to the legs.

Step 13: Glue the head to the neck.

Step 14: Thread the wire down through the legs.

Step 15: Glue the tabs at the top of the body stand to the inside-top of the body. The body should be free to rock on the legs.

Step 16: Glue the link end to the inside-top of the head so that the tab touches the front of the head.

Step 17: Thread the wire down through the large hole in the clothespin and out through the smaller hole. Glue the feet to the clothespin, positioning the moose so that the wire is free to move.

Step 18: Scrape a shallow trough in the clothespin. Bend the wire, and cut it off. Secure the wire with the wire cover. Squeeze the clothespin to make the moose stretch his neck and body.

Growling Bear

An ingenious crank mechanism opens the bear's mouth and raises her arms!
Don't worry, though. The bear is only an inch tall. See page 79.

You will need:

- 1 wooden clothespin
- 2 wire paper clips

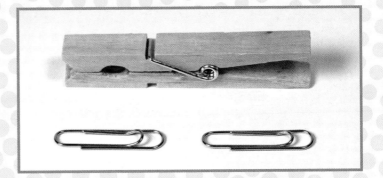

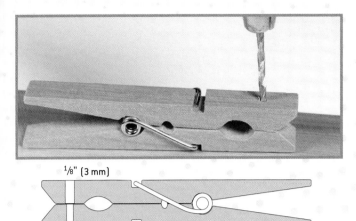

¹/₈" (3 mm)

⁵/₆₄" (2 mm)

Step 1: Use the clothespin template to mark where the hole in the clothespin will go. Place the clothespin on a piece of waste wood so that you do not damage the worktop. Drill down through the clothespin using a 5/64" (2 mm) drill. Drill again, but this time with a 1/8" (3 mm) drill and only through the top jaw of the clothespin.

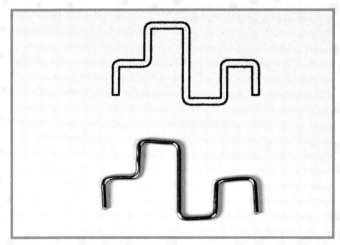

Step 2: Straighten a paper clip, and shape it to match the crank template.

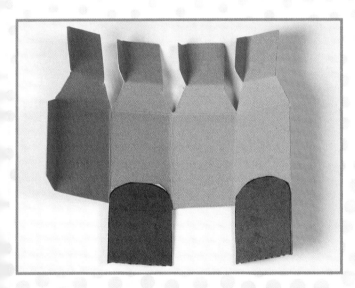

Step 3: Fold up and glue down the long tabs on the body to make a double thickness card for the legs.

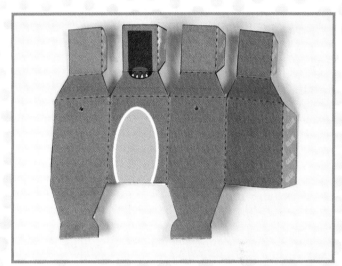

Step 4: Carefully cut out the legs.

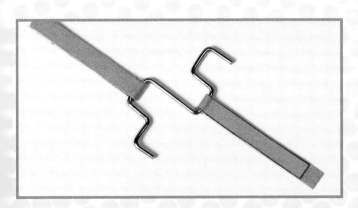

Step 5: Fold the two straps in half, and glue them to the crank.

Step 6: Assemble the head.

Step 7: Glue on the ears and nose.

Step 8: Assemble the head—inner.

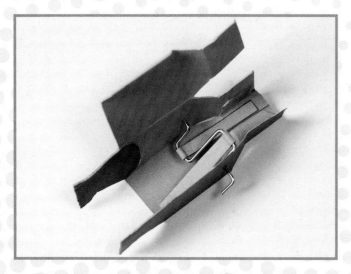

Step 9: Thread the crank through the holes in the side of the body. Arrange the straps with one going up and one going down.

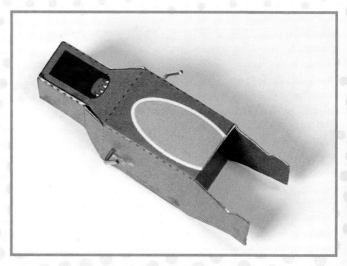

Step 10: Fold around and glue the body.

Step 11: Thread the head—inner down into the body with the top strap inside it.

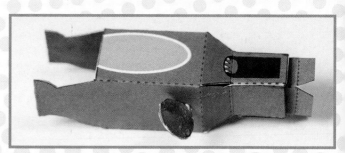

Step 12: Glue the circular shoulder tabs back to back on the two arm wires.

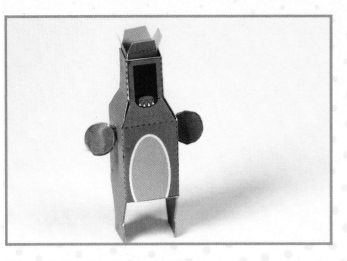

Step 13: With the upward-facing strap at its lowest point, glue it to the inside-back of the head—inner.

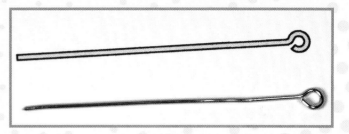

Step 14: Using the template as a guide, straighten and shape a paper clip to make the pull wire.

Step 15: Fold over and glue the tab onto the wire loop.

Step 16: Glue the tab to the downward-facing strap.

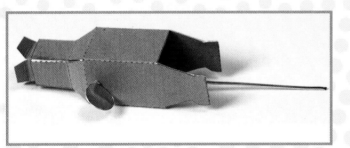

Step 17: As you pull the wire, the shoulder circles should turn and the head—inner should rise.

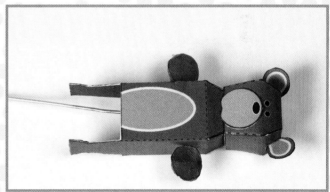

Step 18: Glue the head to the tabs on the top of the head—inner.

Step 19: Glue the arms to the shoulder circles and the paw pads to the back.

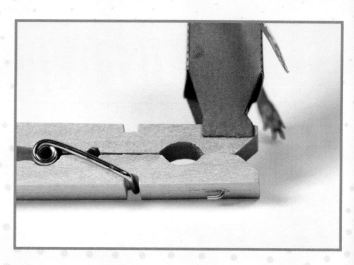

Step 20: Thread the wire down through the large hole in the clothespin and out through the bottom hole. With the arms down, bend the wire to 90° and trim all but about 1/8" (3 mm) from the wire.

Step 21: Scratch a trough for the wire, and fix it into place with the cover piece.

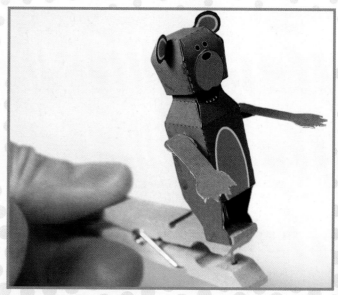

Step 22: Squeeze the clothespin to make the mama bear roar!

Trumpeting Elephant

The hidden pull tab raises the elephant's trunk!
See page 83.

You will need:

- 1 wooden clothespin
- 1 wire paper clip

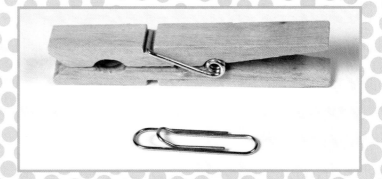

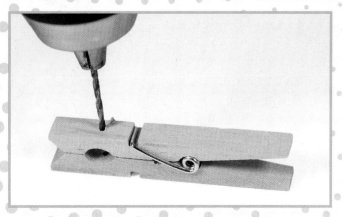

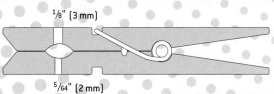

1/8" (3 mm)

5/64" (2 mm)

Step 1: Use the template to mark where the hole in the clothespin will go. Place the clothespin on a piece of waste wood so that you do not damage the worktop. Drill down all the way through the clothespin using a 5/64" (2 mm) drill. Drill again, but this time with a 1/8" (3 mm) drill and only through the top jaw of the clothespin.

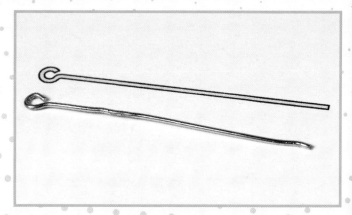

Step 2: Straighten a wire paper clip. Then use a pair of needle-nose pliers to shape it the same as the template. Use wire cutters to cut off any excess wire.

Step 4: Glue together the bell crank.

Step 3: Carefully score all the dotted lines of the parts so that they fold easily. Pre-crease the trunk so that it's ready for assembly.

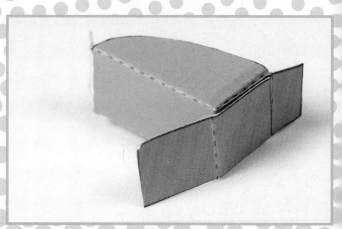

Step 5: Glue the hinge to the base of the bell crank.

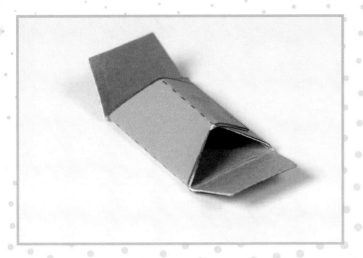

Step 6: Assemble the body base.

Step 7: Glue the body base and the bell crank together.

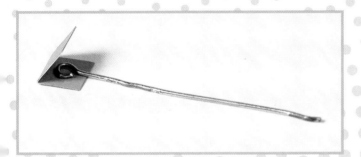

Step 8: Glue the trunk tab over the end of the wire, and glue it down.

Step 9: Squeeze both sides of the tab tight, and let the glue dry.

Step 10: Fold up and glue the sections of the elephant's trunk.

Step 11: Let the glue dry.

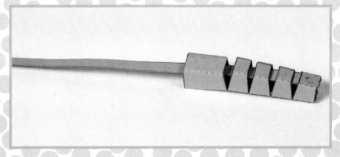

Step 12: Glue the pull tab to the inside-top of the front trunk section.

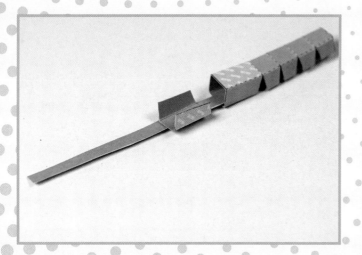

Step 13: Slide the guide over the pull tab.

Step 14: Glue the guide to the inside of the largest trunk section. Make sure the pull tab is free to slide.

Step 15: Glue the trunk to the inside of the head.

Step 16: Here's a view from the front.

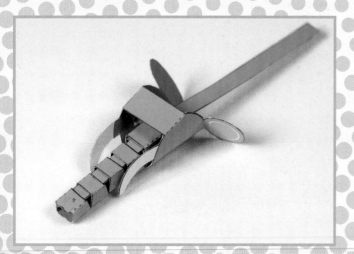

Step 17: Curve the head around, and glue it in place.

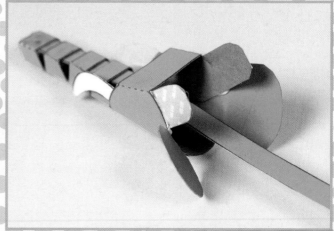

Step 18: Glue the two head supports into place.

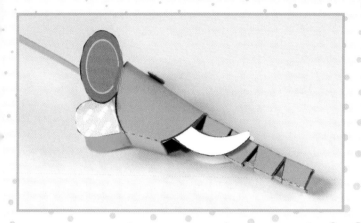

Step 19: Glue on the eyes.

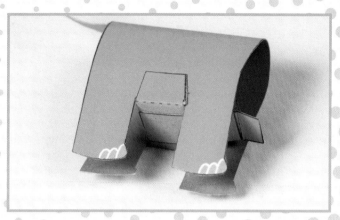

Step 20: Curve the body around. Glue the body and body—inner together. The bell crank should be at the front.

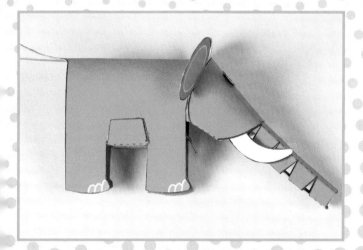

Step 21: Thread the head pull tab through the body and out past the tail, over the top of the bell crank. Glue the head to the body.

Step 22: Move the bell crank so that it is sloping toward the back of the body. Pull the trunk tab so that the trunk is down. Glue the bell crank and trunk pull tab together by the bell crank tab. When the glue is dry, cut off any excess pull tab.

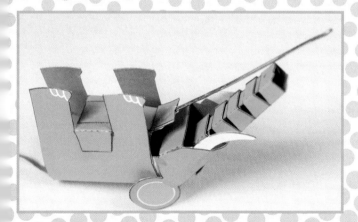

Step 23: Glue the paper tab on the wire to the other end of the bell crank.

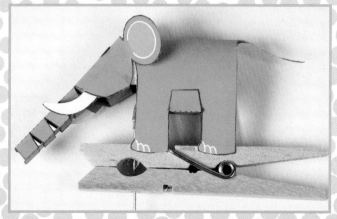

Step 24: Thread the wire down through the hole in the clothespin. Glue the feet to the clothespin.

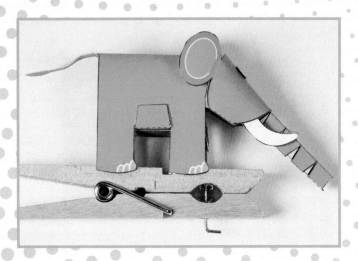

Step 25: With the trunk down, bend the wire and use wire cutters to cut it to make a 3/16" (5 mm) long angle.

Step 26: Cover the wire, and glue it down.

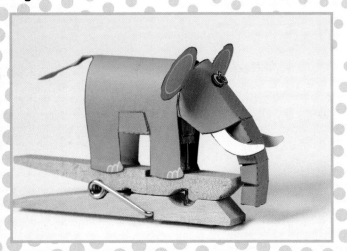

Step 27: Once the glue is dry, the elephant is ready for action!

Step 28: Squeeze the clothespin to raise the trunk.

Roaring T. rex

The tyrant lizard king opens his mouth with a terrifying roar!
Hidden levers and linkages bring this monster to life. See page 85.

You will need:

- 1 wooden clothespin
- 1 wire paper clip

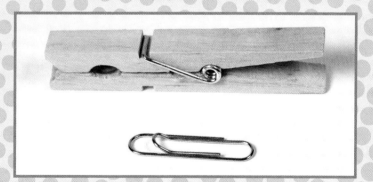

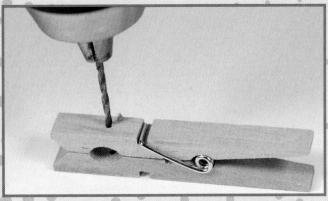

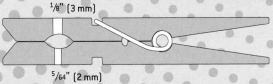

Step 1: Use the template to mark where the hole in the clothespin will go. Place the clothespin on a piece of waste wood so that you do not damage the worktop. Drill down all the way through the clothespin using a 5/64" (2 mm) drill. Drill again, but this time with a 1/8" (3 mm) drill and only through the top jaw of the clothespin.

Step 3: Glue together the feet to make a double thickness card.

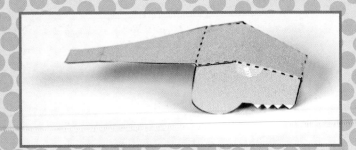

Step 5: Fold up and glue the head.

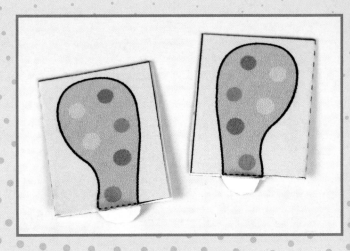

Step 2: Fold the legs in half, and glue them down to make a double thickness card. Don't glue the semicircular tabs together.

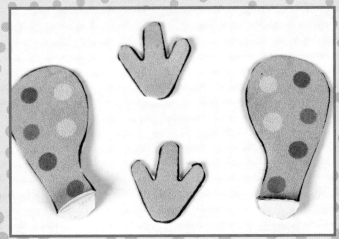

Step 4: Carefully cut out the legs and the feet.

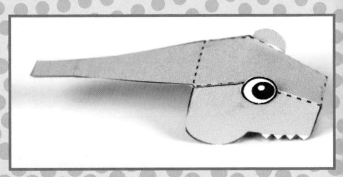

Step 6: Glue the eyes into place.

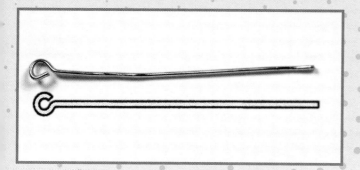

Step 7: Straighten a wire paper clip. Then use a pair of needle-nose pliers to shape it the same as the template. Use wire cutters to cut off any excess wire.

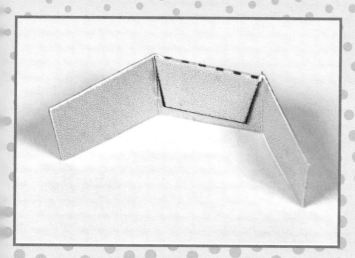

Step 9: Fold down the flap on the head—inner, and glue it into place.

Step 11: Fold over and glue down the side of the head stand piece to make a double thickness card.

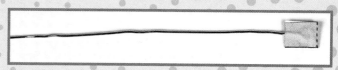

Step 8: Fold the wire end-piece over the circular end of the wire. Pinch it tightly, and allow the glue to dry completely.

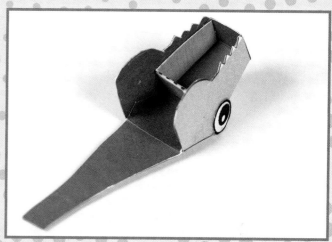

Step 10: Glue the head—inner into the head so that the ends are touching the inside-front of the snout.

Step 12: Glue the head stand tab to the inside of the head.

Step 13: Glue together the lower jaw.

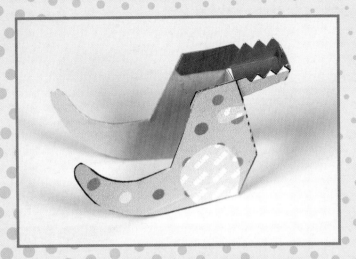

Step 14: Fold the body and glue the lower jaw into place so that it lines up with the top of the body.

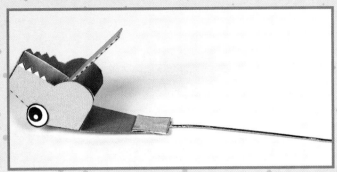

Step 15: Glue the tab on the end of the wire to the long head tab.

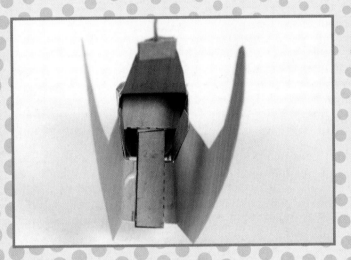

Step 16: Glue the head stand to the inside-front of the body.

Step 17: Here's a side view of the body with the head attached. Pull the wire to make the mouth open and close.

Step 18: Glue the body—back into place, and glue together the ends of the tail.

Step 19: Glue the legs to the feet. Use the picture as a guide to get the feet on correctly!

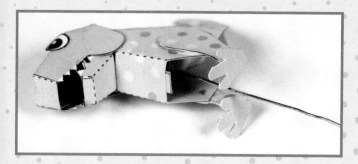

Step 20: Glue the legs to the body.

Step 21: Here's a side view of the body. Pull the wire to make sure the head still works!

Step 22: With the larger hole at the top, thread the wire down through both holes and out the other side.

Step 23: Bend the wire over to 90º, and use wire cutters to cut so that there is a 3/16" (5 mm) angled end. Scrape a shallow trough in the clothespin where the wire will fit snuggly.

Step 24: Glue the clothespin cover over the wire to hold it in place.

Step 25: Admire your handiwork! Squeeze the clothespin to make the T. rex open his mouth and roar!

Paper Animals
IN ACTION!
Model Parts

Talking Triceratops

Head—Top

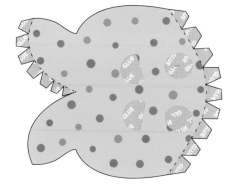

Lower Jaw

Head—Inner

Frill

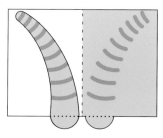

Horn

 Eyes

Tongue

Horn

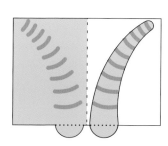

Horn

Flying Pig

Body—Outer

Body—Inner

Wings

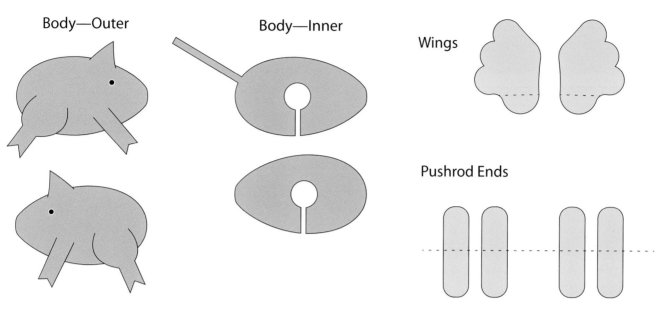

Pushrod Ends

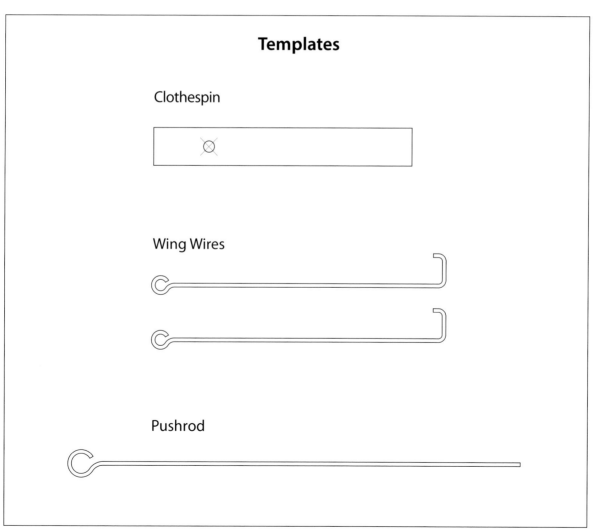

Templates

Clothespin

Wing Wires

Pushrod

Flying Goose

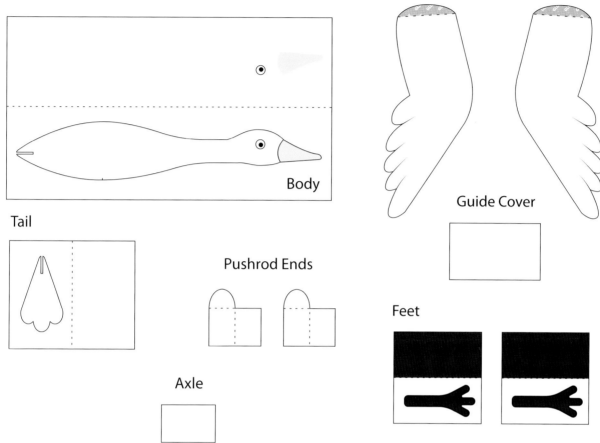

Body

Tail

Guide Cover

Pushrod Ends

Feet

Axle

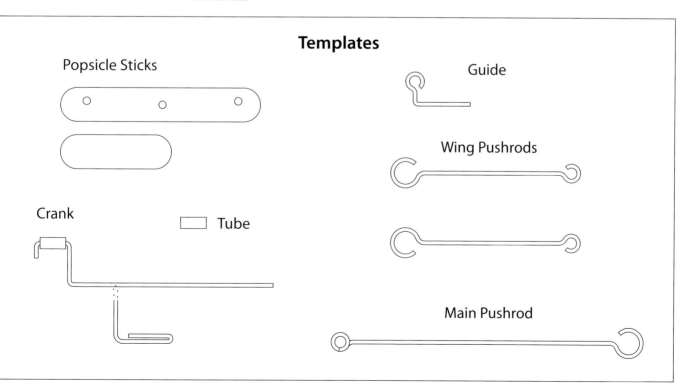

Templates

Popsicle Sticks

Guide

Wing Pushrods

Crank

Tube

Main Pushrod

Nodding Dog

Body

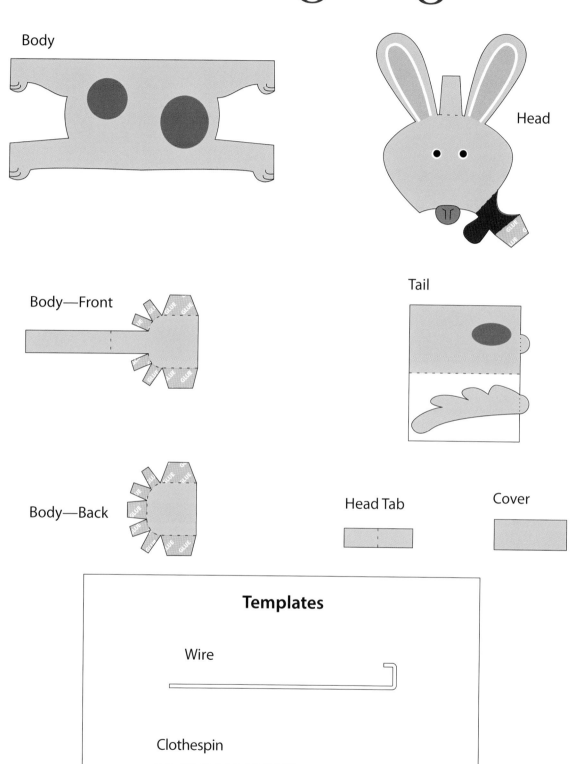

Head

Body—Front

Tail

Body—Back

Head Tab

Cover

Templates

Wire

Clothespin

Pecking Bird

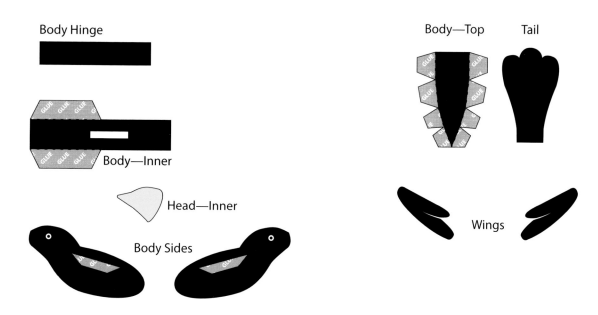

Body Hinge

Body—Inner

Head—Inner

Body Sides

Body—Top

Tail

Wings

Templates

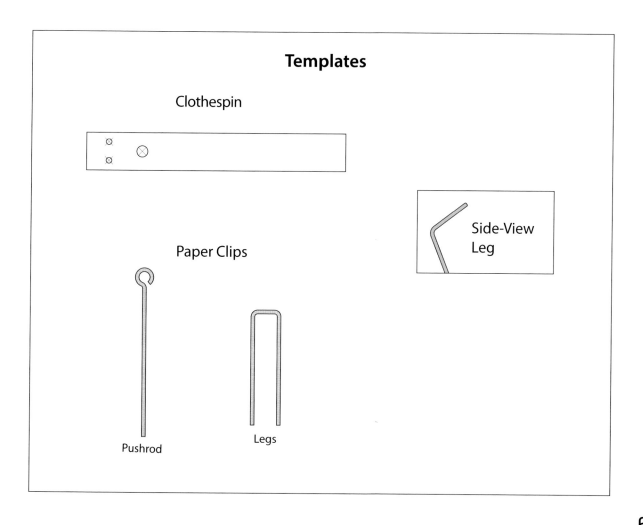

Clothespin

Side-View Leg

Paper Clips

Pushrod

Legs

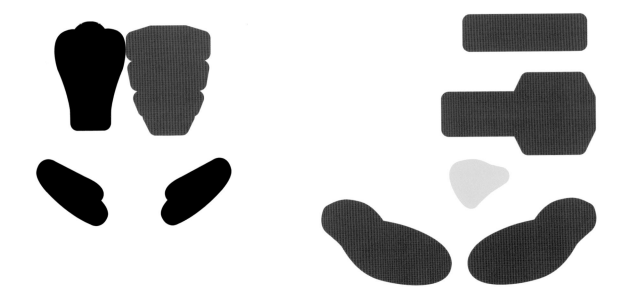

Surprised Penguin

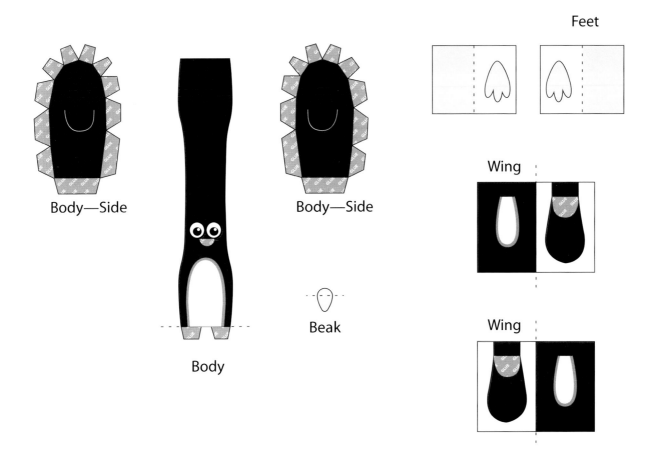

Body—Side

Body

Body—Side

Beak

Feet

Wing

Wing

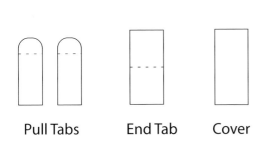

Pull Tabs   End Tab   Cover

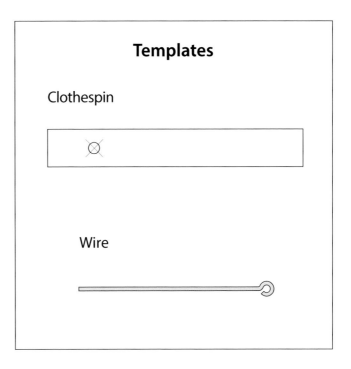

Templates

Clothespin

Wire

Flapping Butterfly

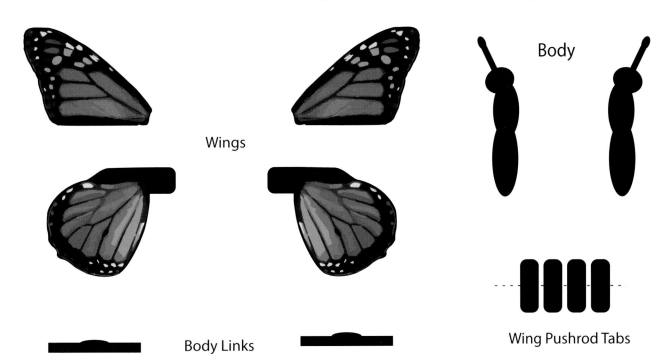

Wings

Body

Body Links

Wing Pushrod Tabs

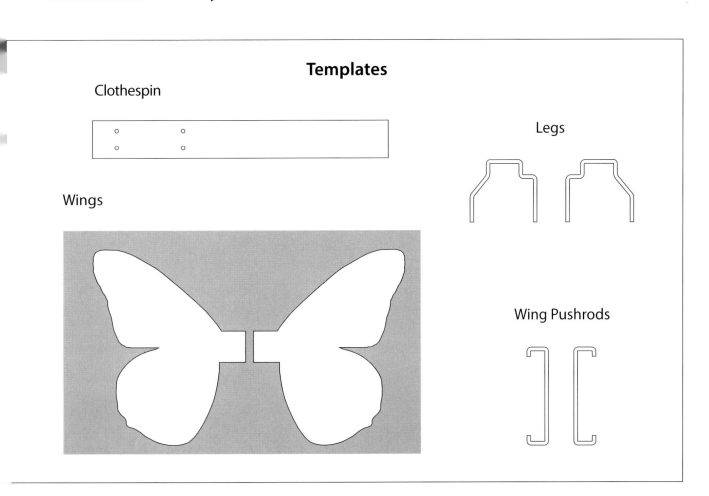

Templates

Clothespin

Wings

Legs

Wing Pushrods

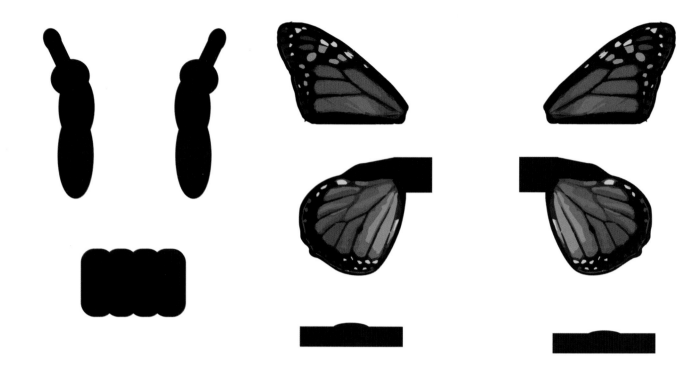

Brave Turtle

Stage One

Stage Two

Head

Base

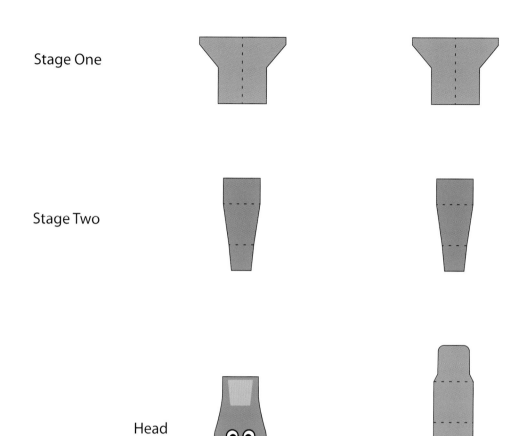

Legs

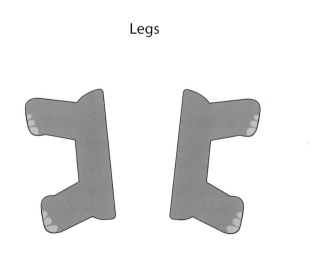

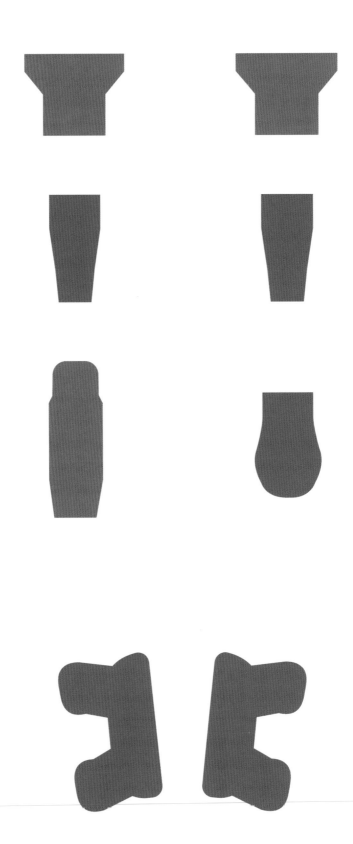

Shell   Wire Cover

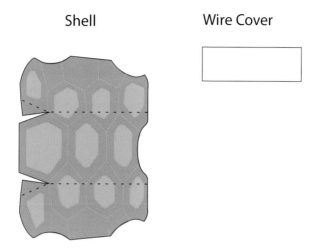

Templates

Clothespin

⊗

Wire

Stretching Moose

Legs

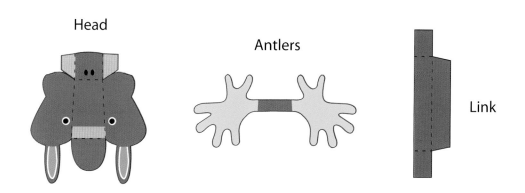

Body Stand

Head

Antlers

Link

Wire End

Wire Cover

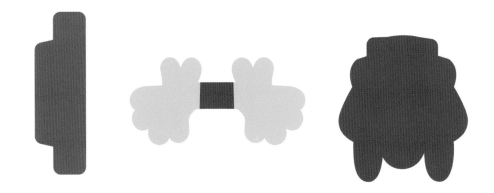

Neck

Body—Outer

Tail

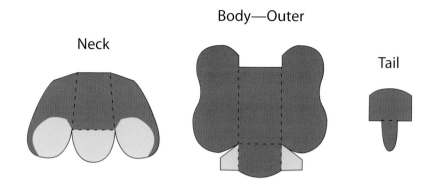

Templates

Clothespin

Pushrod

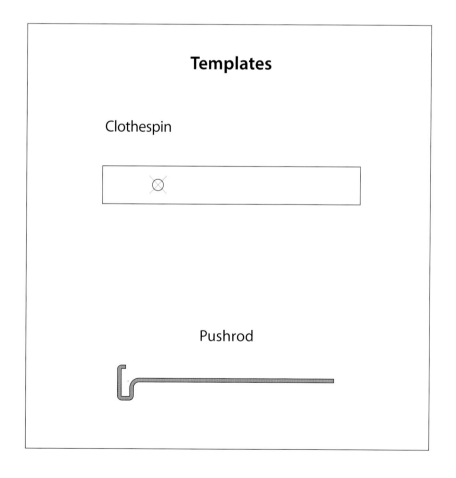

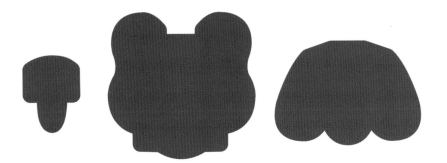

Growling Bear

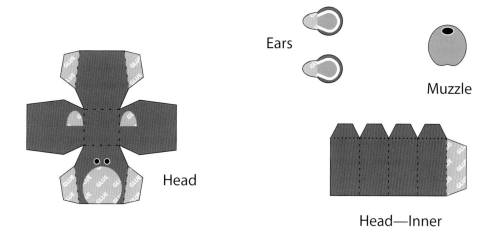

Ears

Muzzle

Head

Head—Inner

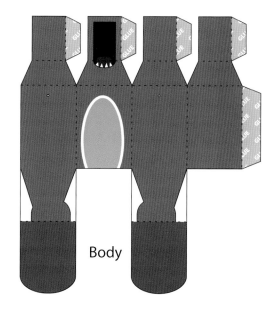

Body

Arms

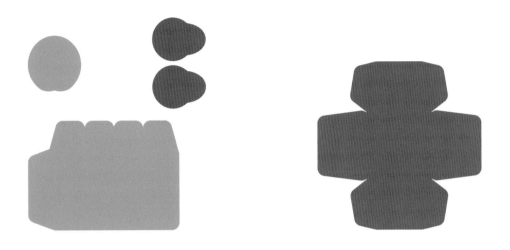

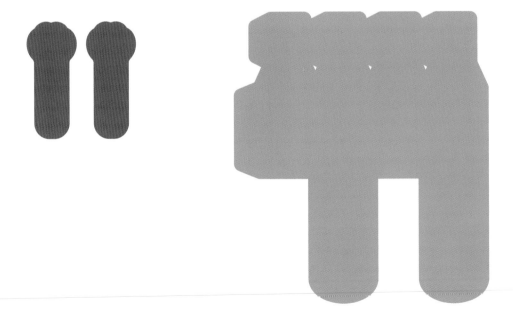

Templates

Pull Wire

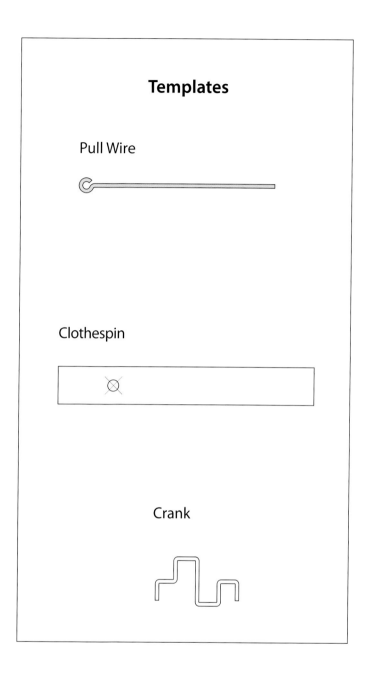

Clothespin

Crank

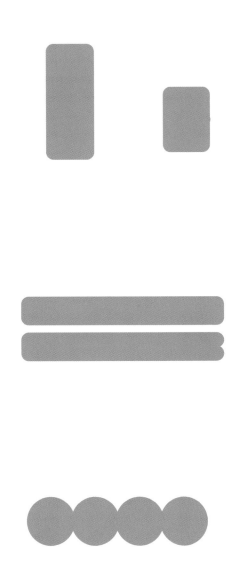

Trumpeting Elephant

Guide

Head Supports

Head

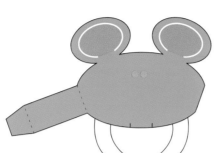

Eyes

Trunk

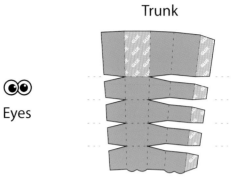

Pull Tab

Body

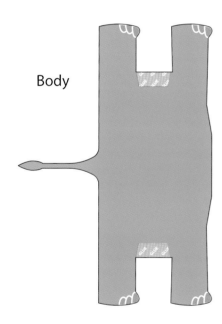

Trunk Tab　　Hinge　　Cover

Bell Crank

Body Base

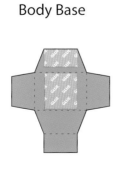

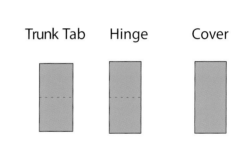

Templates

Clothespin

Pull Wire

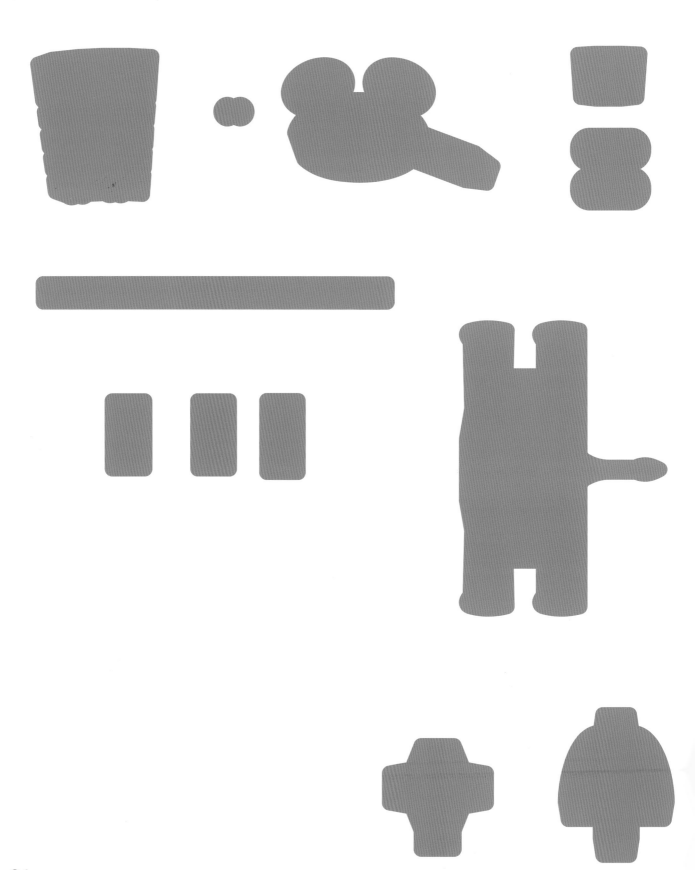

Roaring T. rex

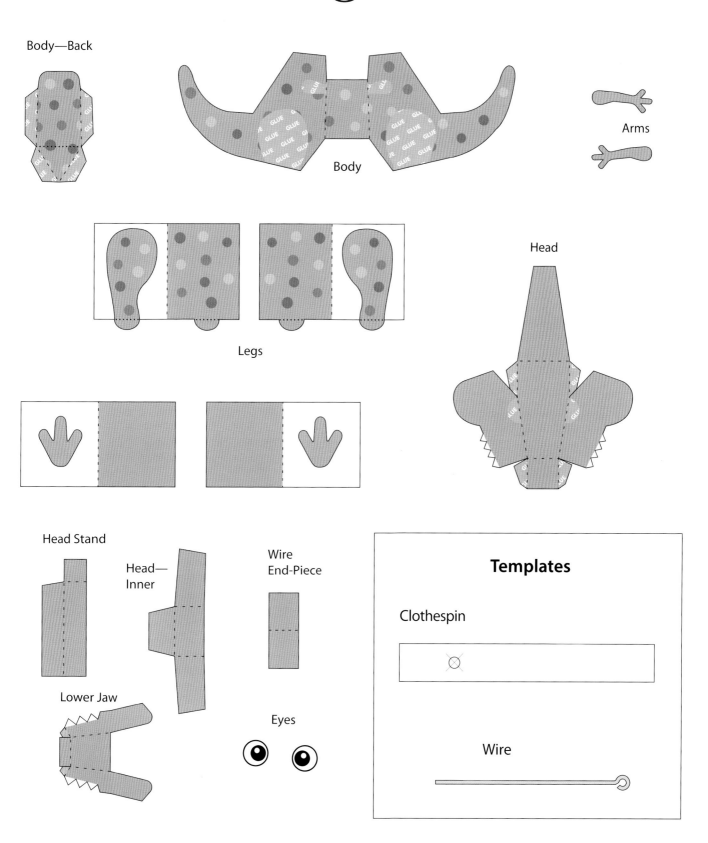

Body—Back

Body

Arms

Legs

Head

Head Stand

Head—
Inner

Wire
End-Piece

Lower Jaw

Eyes

Templates

Clothespin

Wire

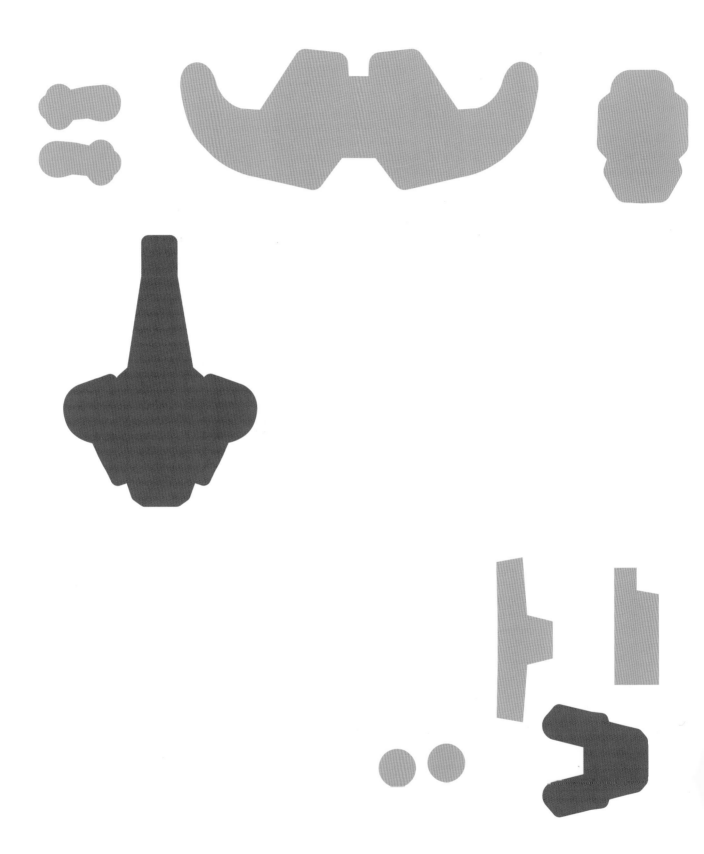